I0036072

Lessons from the Global Laboratory of Economic Experimentation

Selected essays

Dan Mitchell

LibertyFest, Brisbane
Monograph 1

Connor Court Publishing

Connor Court Publishing Pty Ltd
PO Box 7257
Redland Bay QLD 4165
sales@connorcourt.com
www.connorcourt.com

Phone 0497 900 685

ISBN: 978-1-925501-67-4

Cover design: Maria Giordano

Printed in Australia

Distributed in Australia by Brumby SunState and Connor Court Publishing

Distributed in the UK, Europe, and North America by Ingram Inc.

LibertyFest Monographs

LibertyFest is conceived as a series of annual conferences celebrating and honouring the very idea of liberty. Ideas such as all individuals being free to enjoy their natural rights to life, liberty and property. That each of us should be free to live our lives in the manner that suits us provided we respect the equal rights of others to do the same. The idea that the rule of common law and enforcement can be used to protect people's natural rights but that state enforcement should not be used to coerce people into things they do not care for. The idea that we each have the ability to exercise free will and in doing so will take responsibility for the consequences of our actions.

These ideas are not new, they emerged from the writings of classical liberal economists and libertarian philosophers over many centuries. However, in recent times these ideas are gradually being eroded and diluted as interventionist fads take hold at both a governmental level and among the voting public. The arguments for free markets, smaller government and less tax are having to be remade to new generations which is why Connor Court and LibertyFest have created the LibertyFest Series of Monographs drawn from selected LibertyFest speakers.

Lessons from the Global Laboratory of Economic Experimentation is our first Monograph in this series, written by well-known and popular American economist Dan Mitchell. Dan is one of a small number of economists prepared to take their arguments to the people directly, to demonstrate the positive impacts of free markets and lower taxation and to reject the big government economics that dominates public discourse today. Connor Court Publishing and LibertyFest are proud to have Dan Mitchell in Australia, to provide a forum at our conference for him to share his ideas and to support him by publishing this monograph. We hope you support Dan and his ideas too.

LibertyFest conferences exist to give a voice and a outlet for liberty loving ideas. When you read this book and attend a LibertyFest conference our hope is you do this with an open mind. Open to learning something new and being prepared to shoulder a small amount of responsibility to help spread these ideas among your friends. The future may depend upon it.

Andrew Cooper, Director

LibertyFest, Brisbane

TABLE OF CONTENTS

INTRODUCTION

The world can be viewed as an ongoing series of economic experiments. Some nations have high taxes while other have low taxes. Some countries have lots of regulation, some are more laissez-faire in their orientation. Jurisdictions also have different approaches on monetary policy, trade policy, government spending, and labor policy. Pick any issue, and you will be able to find governments across the globe with different approaches.

When looking at the relative economic performance of various nations, what can we learn about the desirability of various policies?

We can draw easy conclusions by looking at extreme examples. Hong Kong and Singapore, for instance, normally rank very high for pro-market policies. And they also enjoy a great deal of prosperity and rapid growth. Nations such as Venezuela and North Korea, by contrast, stand out for pervasive statism. And they suffer from widespread misery, with high levels of poverty and economic stagnation.

In other cases, it's more complex. In the Nordic nations, taxes are high and the welfare state is large, yet these countries tend to be very pro-free market in other policy areas. So which policies should get the credit (or the blame) if the economy does well (or does poorly)?

On the other hand, the fiscal burden of government is small in many developing nations, yet those also are the places that are infamous for heavy regulation and rampant government corruption.

What policies deserve credit if a developing nation is growing and – hopefully – converging with the western world? And what policies deserve blame if a developing nation remains poor and economically backwards?

From a big-picture perspective, it's helpful to peruse *Economic Freedom of the World*, published by the Fraser Institute in Canada. That annual document measures economic liberty based on how governments deal with five major issues: fiscal policy, trade policy, regulatory policy, monetary policy, and rule of law. I always think of this publication as a report card. Nations get separate grades for the five areas and their total score is akin to a grade point average.

But it's also helpful to examine specific policy reforms on a country-by-country basis. My daily columns frequently cite a jurisdiction's score from *Economic Freedom of the World*, but usually as part of a discussion about some change – for better or worse – in a particular issue area. Are tax rates increasing or decreasing? Is red tape expanding or contracting?

By writing about developments all over the world, the goal is to show policymakers real-world examples of how nations get good results of bad results based on what's happening to the overall level of government involvement in economic affairs.

The good news, at least for those who favor economic liberty, is that the global experiment teaches a very consistent lesson about the comparative merits of free enterprise and economic liberty. There is a strong relationship between pro-market policies and better economic performance.

Since I'm first and foremost a public finance economist, I'll share one of my favorite tactics when debating fiscal policy. I'll oftentimes share a table (see next page) showing a list of nations that have achieved very good results by restraining the growth of government spending. I'll show how the burden of government spending declined as a share of economic output and I'll show how budget deficits also shrank as a share of GDP. I'll then ask my colleague from the other side to please share a list of nations that got good results by raising taxes. Unsurprisingly, the usual response is either untrue claims or hemming and hawing.

When seeking to educate and convince a non-ideological audience that they should favor economic freedom, I've learned that there's no substitute for this kind of real-world evidence. Most people think of themselves as being practical. My daily columns are designed to reach these people. If I can reach their minds, maybe their hearts will follow.

Nation	Years	Average Annual Spending Growth	Change in burden of Government/GDP	Change in Deficit/GDP
Ireland	1985-1989	1.5%	-12.2%	-9.9%
New Zealand	1991-1997	0.5%	-11.0%	- 5.8%
Sweden	1992-2001	1.9%	-15.0%	-10.5%
Canada	1992-1997	0.8%	-9.4%	-9.3%
Netherlands	1995-2000	1.5%	-5.2%	-3.8%
Italy	1996-2000	1.1%	-6.2%	-6.0%
Singapore	1998-2007	-1.1%	-15.9%	-10.4%
Slovakia	2000-2004	1.3%	-14.5%	-9.9%
Taiwan	2001-2006	-0.6%	-5.9%	-7.0%
Israel	2002-2005	0.8%	-5.7%	-2.7%
Germany	2003-2007	0.2%	-5.4%	-4.3%
Switzerland	2004-Present	1.9%	-3.2%	-1.4%
Estonia	2008-2011	1.1%	-5.4%	-4.3%
Lithuania	2008-2012	0.8%	+1.3%	-0.4%
Latvia	2008-Present	-4.2%	-7.1%	-7.0%
Iceland	2009-Present	1.9%	-6.7%	-6.8%

Source: IMF World Economic Outlook database, spending at all levels of government.

RIGHT, LEFT, FACTS, AND VALUES

August 19, 2017

Since my job is to proselytize on behalf of economic liberty, I'm always trying to figure out what motivates people. To be blunt, I'll hopefully be more effective if I understand how they decide what policies to support. That's a challenge when dealing with my friends on the left since some of them seem to be motivated by envy.

Unsurprisingly, there are people on the other side who also contemplate how to convert their opponents.

Harvard Professor Maximilian Kasy wrote a column for the *Washington Post* that advises folks on the left how they can be more effective when arguing with folks on the right. He starts with an assertion that conservatives are basically impervious to facts.

> Worries about…our "post-factual era" impeding political debate in our society have become commonplace. Liberals…are often astonished at the seeming indifference of their opponents toward facts and toward the likely consequences of political decisions. …A common, though apparently ineffective, response to this frustration is to double down by discussing more facts.

This is a remarkable assertion. I'm a libertarian rather than a conservative, so I don't feel personally insulted. That being said, conservatives generally are my allies on economic issues and I've never found them to be oblivious or indifferent to facts (I'm speaking about policy wonks, not politicians, who often are untethered from reality regardless of their ideology).

So let's see how Mr. Kasy justifies his claim about conservatives. Here's more of what he wrote.

> ...maybe the issue is not conservatives' ignorance of facts, but rather a fundamental difference of values. Taking this point of view seems essential for effective communication across the political divide.

I basically agree that differences in values play a big role, so I'm sort of okay with that part of his analysis (I'll return to this issue in the conclusion).

But my alarm bells started ringing at this next passage.

> Much normative (or value-based) reasoning by liberals (and mainstream economists) is about the *consequences* of political actions for the welfare of individuals. Statements about the desirability of policies are based on trading off the consequences for different individuals. If good outcomes result from a policy without many negative consequences, then the policy is a good one.

Huh? Since when are liberals (and he's talking about today's statists, not the classical liberals of yesteryear) and mainstream economists on the same side?

Though I admit it's hard to argue about the rule he proposes for policy. He's basically saying that a change is desirable if "good outcomes" are more prevalent than "negative consequences."

That's probably too utilitarian for me, but I suspect most people might agree with that approach.

But he makes a giant and unsubstantiated leap by then claiming it would be wrong to repeal a supposedly good policy like Obamacare.

> When Sen. Kamala D. Harris (D-Calif.) remarked on the Affordable Care Act this spring, for example, she said, "...we're talking about something that would deny those in need with the relief and the

help that they need, that they want and deserve…" In other words, if a policy will harm the welfare of individuals in need, it's a bad policy.

Huh? What happened to his utilitarian formula about "good outcomes" vs "negative consequences"? Sure, some additional people have health insurance coverage, but is he blind to rising premiums, job losses, higher taxes, loss of plans and loss of doctors, dumping people into Medicaid, and other downsides of Obamacare?

If facts are important, shouldn't he be weighing the costs and benefits?

In other words, Kasy must be in some sort of cocoon if he thinks the Obamacare fight is between Republicans motivated only by values and Democrats motivated by helping individuals.

His analysis of the death tax is similarly off base.

> …consider the example of bequest taxes, labeled "estate taxes" by liberals and "death taxes" by conservatives. A liberal might invoke various empirical facts…our empiricist liberal might conclude that bequest taxes are an effective policy instrument, providing public revenue and promoting equality of opportunity. The conservative addressee of these facts might now just shrug her shoulders and say "no thanks." Our conservative likely believes that everyone has the right to keep the fruits of her labor, and free contracts of exchange between any two parties are nobody else's business. …Taxing bequests thus means punishing moral behavior, the exact *opposite* of what the government should do.

Once again, Kasy is deluding himself. Conservatives do think the death tax is morally wrong, so he's right about that, but they also have very compelling arguments about the levy's negative economic impact. Simply stated, the death tax exacerbates the tax code's bias against capital formation and results in all sorts of economically inefficient tax avoidance behavior (with Bill and Hillary Clinton being classic examples).

His column concludes with some suggestions of how folks on the left can be more persuasive. He basically says they should appeal to conservatives with values-based arguments such as these.

> We should evaluate the policy based on its effect on individuals, and assign a higher weight to the majority of less wealthy people. ...nobody can be said to consume only the products of their own labor. We rely on social institutions including markets and governments to provide us with all the goods we consume, and absent a theory of just prices (which present day conservatives don't have) there is no sense in which we are entitled to specific terms of exchange.

I'm not the ideal person to speak for conservatives, but I don't think those arguments will win many converts.

Regarding his first suggestion, Kasy's problem is that he apparently assumes that people on the right don't care about the poor. Maybe I'm reading between the lines, but he seems to think conservatives will automatically favor lots of redistribution if he can convince that it's good to help the poor.

I think it's much more accurate to assume that plenty of conservatives have thought about how to help the poor, but they've concluded that the welfare state is injurious and that it is more effective to focus on policies such as school choice, economic growth, and occupational licensing.

Indeed, I hope most conservatives would agree with my Bleeding Heart Rule.

And his second idea is even stranger because economic

conservatives have a theory of just prices. It's whatever emerges from competitive markets.

Let's close with a column by Alberto Mingardi of the Bruno Leoni Institute in Italy. Published by the Foundation for Economic Education, the piece is relevant to today's topic since it looks at why an unfortunate number of intellectuals are opposed to economic liberty.

> ...some have replied that the main reason is resentment (intellectuals expect more recognition from the market society than they actually get); some have pointed out that self-interest drives the phenomenon (intellectuals preach government controls and regulation because they'll be the controllers and regulators); some have taken the charitable view that intellectuals do not understand what the market really is about (as they cherish "projects" and the market is instead an unplanned order).

Alberto then shares Milton Friedman's answer.

> I think a major reason why intellectuals tend to move towards collectivism is that the collectivist answer is a simple one. If there's something wrong pass a law and do something about it. If there's something wrong it's because of some no-good bum, some devil, evil and wicked – that's a very simple story to tell. You don't have to be very smart to write it and you don't have to be very smart to accept it.

My two cents, based on plenty of conversations with well-meaning folks on the left, is that there's actually a lot of agreement of some big-picture values. We all want less poverty and more prosperity. In other words, I think most people have similar good intentions (I'm obviously excluding communists, Nazis, and others who believe in totalitarianism).

But similar good intentions doesn't translate into agreement on policy because of secondary values. Especially differences in whether we view "equality of outcomes" as an appropriate goal for government. Some on the left openly are willing to sacrifice growth to achieve more equality (Margaret Thatcher even claimed that they would be willing to hurt the poor if the rich suffered even more). Folks on the right, by contrast, are much more focused on helping the poor with growth rather than redistribution.

Because Protecting the Environment Is Important, Capitalism Should Play a Bigger Role

August 16, 2017

Over the years, I've had fun mocking the silly extremism of the environmental movement.

- Some environmentalists don't believe in bathing,

- How about the environmentalists who sterilize themselves to avoid carbon-producing children,

- Or consider the environmentalists who produce/use hand-cranked vibrators to reduce their carbon footprint.

- There are also environmentalist who claim that climate change causes AIDS.

- Environmentalists assert that you're racist if you oppose their agenda.

- And environmentalists put together a ranking implying that Cuba is better than the United States.

- The environmentalists who choose death to lower their carbon footprints.

That being said, protecting the environment is a worthy and important goal.

And that's why some of us want to give the private sector a bigger role.

John Stossel, for instance, has a must-watch video on how capitalism can save endangered rhinos.

Professor Philip Booth expands on the lesson in the video and urges broad application of market forces to preserve the environment.

Especially well-enforced property rights.

> …what is needed for better husbandry of ecological resources is more widespread and deeper establishment of property rights together with their enforcement. The cause of environmentalism is often associated with the Left. This is despite the fact that some of the worst environmental outcomes in the history of our planet have been associated with Communist governments. …a great deal of serious work has been produced by those who believe in market or community-based solutions to environmental problems, and a relatively small role for government. For example, Ronald Coase and Elinor Ostrom are two Nobel Prize winners in economics who have made profound contributions to our understanding of how markets and communities can promote environmental conservation. Indeed, the intellectual and moral high ground when it comes to environmentalism ought to be taken by those who believe in private property, strong community institutions and a free economy.

Philip explains why private ownership produces conservation.

> If things are owned, they will tend to be looked after. The owner of a lake will not fish it to near extinction (or even over-fish the lake to a small degree) because the breeding potential of the fish would be reduced.

He then explains the downside of public ownership.

On the other hand, if the lake is not owned by anybody, or if it is owned by the government and fishing is unregulated, the lake will be fished to extinction because nobody has any benefit from holding back. Local businesses may well also pollute the lake if there are no well-defined ownership rights. The much-cited work here is Hardin's *Tragedy of the Commons* (1968), though, in fact, Hardin was simply referring back to a pamphlet by William Forster Lloyd which was written in 1833. In that pamphlet, a situation was described whereby common land was open to grazing by all. The land would then be over-grazed because a person would get the benefit of putting additional cattle on the land without the cost that arises from over-grazing which would be shared by all users.

He points out that one advantage of Brexit is that the U.K. can implement a fisheries system based on property rights.

Now that fishing policy has been repatriated, the UK should establish property rights in sea fisheries. Few would seriously question private property when it comes to the land. For example, it is rare these days to find people who would suggest that farms should be nationalised or collectivised or returned to an unregulated commons where anybody can graze their animals without restriction. It would be understood that this would lead to chaos, inefficiency and environmental catastrophe.

And since we have real-world evidence that fisheries based on property rights are very successful, hopefully the U.K. government will implement this reform.

So what's the bottom line on capitalism and the environment?

If we want sustainable environmental outcomes, the answer almost never lies with government control, but with the establishment and enforcement of property rights over environmental resources. This provides the incentive to nurture and conserve. Where the government does intervene it should try to mimic markets. When it comes to the environment, misguided government intervention can lead to conflict and poor environmental outcomes. The best thing the government can do is put its own house in order and ensure that property rights are enforced through proper policing and courts systems. That is certainly the experience of forested areas in South America.

Let's close by noting one other reason to give the market a bigger role. Simply stated, environmentalists seem to have no sense of cost-benefit analysis. Instead, we get bizarre policies that seem motivated primarily by virtue signalling.

- The environmentalist-driven war on high-quality light bulbs.

- The environmentalist-driven rule against working toilets.

- The environmentalist-driven prohibition against washing machines that actually clean.

- The environmentalist-driven campaign to eliminate effective showerheads.

- The environmentalist-driven pointless recycling mandates.

And don't forget green energy programs, which impose heavy costs on consumers and also are a combination of virtue signalling and cronyism.

No wonder many of us don't trust the left on global warming, even if we recognize it may be a real issue.

THE NANNY STATE, SHOWERHEADS, AND THE DECLINING QUALITY OF LIFE

JUNE 19, 2017

When I write about regulation, I usually focus on big-picture issues involving economic costs, living standards, and competitiveness.

Those are very important concerns, but the average person in American probably gets more irked by rules that impact the quality of life.

- Inferior light bulbs

- Substandard toilets

- Inadequate washing machines

- Crummy dishwashers

That's a grim list, but it's time to augment it.

Jeffrey Tucker of the Foundation for Economic Education explains that the government also has made showering a less pleasant experience. He starts by expressing envy about Brazilian showers.

> …was shocked with delight at the shower in Brazil. …step into the shower and you have a glorious capitalist experience. Hot water, really hot, pours down on you like a mighty and unending waterfall… At least the socialists in Brazil knew better than to destroy such an essential of civilized life.

I know what he's talking about.

I'm in a hotel (not in Brazil), and my shower this morning was a tedious experience because the water flow was so anemic.

Why would a hotel not want customers to have an enjoyable and quick shower?

The answer is government.

> …here we've forgotten. We have long lived with regulated showers, plugged up with a stopper imposed by government controls imposed in 1992. There was no public announcement. It just happened gradually. After a few years, you couldn't buy a decent shower head. They called it a flow restrictor and said it would increase efficiency. By efficiency, the government means "doesn't work as well as it used to." …You can see the evidence of the bureaucrat in your shower if you pull off the showerhead and look inside. It has all this complicated stuff inside, whereas it should just be an open hole, you know, so the water could get through. The flow stopper is mandated by the federal government.

The problem isn't just the water coming out of the showerhead. It's the water coming into your home.

> It's not just about the showerhead. The water pressure in our homes and apartments has been gradually getting worse for two decades, thanks to EPA mandates on state and local governments. This has meant that even with a good showerhead, the shower is not as good as it might be. It also means that less water is running through our pipes, causing lines to clog and homes to stink just slightly like the sewer. This problem is much more difficult to fix, especially because plumbers are forbidden by law from hacking your water pressure.

So why are politicians and bureaucrats imposing these rules?

Ostensibly for purposes of conservation.

...what about the need to conserve water? Well, the Department of the Interior says that domestic water use, which includes even the water you use on your lawn and flower beds, constitutes a mere 2% of the total, so this unrelenting misery spread by government regulations makes hardly a dent in the whole. In any case, what is the point of some vague sense of "conserving" when the whole purpose of modern appliances and indoor plumbing is to improve our lives and sanitation? (Free societies have a method for knowing how much of something to use or not use; it is called the signaling system of prices.)

Jeffrey is right. If there really is a water shortage (as there sometimes is in parts of the country and world), then prices are the best way of encouraging conservation.

Now let's dig in the archives of the *Wall Street Journal* for a 2010 column on the showerhead issue.

Apparently bureaucrats are irked that builders and consumers used multiple showerheads to boost the quality of their daily showers.

Regulators are going after some of the luxury shower fixtures that took off in the housing boom. Many have multiple nozzles, cost thousands of dollars and emit as many as 12 gallons of water a minute. In May, the DOE stunned the plumbing-products industry when it said it would adopt a strict definition of the term "showerhead"... A 1992 federal law says a showerhead can deliver no more than 2.5 gallons per minute at a flowing water pressure of 80 pounds per square inch. For years, the term "showerhead" in federal regulations was understood by many manufacturers to mean a device that directs water onto a bather. Each nozzle in a shower was considered separate and in compliance if it delivered no more than the 2.5-gallon maximum. But in May, the DOE said a "showerhead" may incorporate "one or more sprays, nozzles or openings." Under the new interpretation, all nozzles would count as a single showerhead and be deemed noncompliant if, taken together, they exceed the 2.5 gallons-a-minute maximum.

And here's something that's both amusing and depressing.

The regulations are so crazy that an entrepreneur didn't think they were real.

> Altmans Products, a U.S. unit of Grupo Helvex of Mexico City, says it got a letter from the DOE in January and has stopped selling several popular models, including the Shower Rose, which delivers 12 gallons of water a minute. Pedro Mier, the firm's vice president, says his customers "just like to feel they're getting a lot of water." Until getting the DOE letter, his firm didn't know U.S. law limited showerhead water usage, Mr. Mier says. "At first, I thought it was a scam."

Unsurprisingly, California is "leading" the way. Here are some passages from an article in the *L.A. Times* from almost two years ago.

> The flow of water from shower heads and bathroom faucets in California will be sharply reduced under strict new limits approved Wednesday by the state Energy Commission. Current rules, established in 1994 at the federal level, allow a maximum flow of 2.5 gallons per minute from a shower head. Effective next July, the limit will fall to 2.0 gallons per minute and will be reduced again in July 2018, to 1.8 gallons, giving California the toughest standard of any U.S. state.

Though "toughest standard" is the wrong way to describe what's happening. It's actually the "worst shower" of any state.

THE RADICAL ENVIRONMENTAL AGENDA SHOULD BE REJECTED, EVEN IF GLOBAL WARMING IS REAL

SEPTEMBER 26, 2014

I believe that protecting the environment is both a good thing and a legitimate function of government.

But I'm rational. So while I want limits on pollution, such policies should be determined by cost-benefit analysis.

Banning automobiles doubtlessly would reduce pollution, for instance, but the economic cost would be catastrophic.

On the other hand, it's good to limit carcinogens from being dumped in the air and water. So long as there's some unbiased science showing net benefits.

But while I'm pro-environment, I'm anti-environmentalist. Simply stated, too many of these people are nuts.

Environmentalists assert that you're racist if you oppose their agenda.

Some environmentalists don't believe in bathing,

How about the environmentalists who sterilize themselves to avoid carbon-producing children,

Or consider the environmentalists who produce/use hand-cranked vibrators to reduce their carbon footprint.

There are also environmentalist who claim that climate change causes AIDS.

And environmentalists put together a ranking implying that Cuba is better than the United States.

Then there's the super-nutty category.

The environmentalists who choose death to lower their carbon footprints.

But since I'm an economist, what really worries me is that these people are statists. There's an old joke that environmentalists are "watermelons" since they're green on the outside and red on the inside.

But maybe it's not really a joke. At least not in all cases. In this video from *Reason*, filmed at the so-called climate march in New York City.

Just in case you think the folks at *Reason* deliberately sought out a few crazy people in an otherwise rational crowd, let's now look at the views of Naomi Klein, who is ostensibly a big thinker for the left on environmental issues.

Slate published an interview with her and you can judge for yourself whether her views are sensible. Here's some of what *Slate* said about her.

> According to social activist and perennial agitator Naomi Klein, the really inconvenient truth about climate change is that it's not about carbon—it's about capitalism. ...she's turned her argument into a hefty book... *This Changes Everything: Capitalism vs. the Climate* is focused on exposing how the relentless pursuit of growth has locked us in to a system that's incompatible with a stable climate. ...

And here's some of what Ms. Klein said.

> The post-carbon economy we can build will have to be better designed. ...not only does climate action mean a healthy community—it's also the best chance at tacking inequality. ... The divestment movement is a start at challenging the excesses of capitalism. It's working to delegitimize fossil fuels, and showing that they're just as unethical as profits from the tobacco industry. ...profits are not legitimate in an era of climate change.

Profits are not legitimate?!? Geesh, sounds like a certain President who also disdains profit.

By the way, I'd bet Naomi Klein has a far bigger "carbon footprint" than the average person.

And I can say with great certainty that other leftists are huge hypocrites on the issue. Check out the vapid actor who did some moral preening at the climate-change march.

Kudos to Ms. Fields. She has a way of exposing phonies on camera.

Though I think it's safe to say that Mr. DiCaprio doesn't win the prize for being the biggest environmental hypocrite.

Shifting back to policy issues, even "mainstream" environmental initiatives are often very misguided. Here are a few examples.

- The environmentalist-driven war on high-quality light bulbs.

- The environmentalist-driven rule against working toilets.

- The environmentalist-driven prohibition against washing machines that actually clean.

- This environmentalist-driven example of EPA thuggery.

- The environmentalist-driven pointless recycling mandates.

The bottom line is that we presumably have some environmental challenges. For instance, it's quite possible that there is some global warming caused by mankind.

I just don't trust environmentalists to make policy. When they're in charge, we get really dumb policies. Or grotesque examples of government thuggery. Or sleazy corruption and cronyism.
But at least we have some decent environmental humor.

Examples of Terrorism Subsidized by Government Handouts

May 29, 2017

Whenever there's a terrorist attack, I automatically feel a combination of anger, horror, and sadness. Like all normal people.

But it's then just a matter of time before I also begin wonder whether we'll learn that the dirtbag terrorist was financed by welfare.

Which is an understandable reaction since that's now the normal pattern. Over and over again, we learn that taxpayers were supporting these murderous losers while they plotted and planned their mayhem.

And it's not random. They're actually told by hate-filled Imams to sign up for handouts. And European courts protect terrorist households that use welfare to finance death and destruction.

It's gotten to the point where I even created a special terror wing in the Moocher Hall of Fame.

And it's happened again. The piece of human filth who murdered 22 people at a concert in Manchester was able to finance his terrorism with handouts from the British government.

The *Telegraph* has some of the odious details about tax-financed death and destruction.

> Salman Abedi is understood to have received thousands of pounds in state funding in the run up to Monday's atrocity even while he was overseas receiving bomb-making training. Police are

28

investigating Abedi's finances, including how he paid for frequent trips to Libya where he is thought to have been taught to make bombs at a jihadist training camp. …Abedi's finances are a major 'theme' of the police inquiry amid growing alarm over the ease with which jihadists are able to manipulate Britain's welfare and student loans system to secure financing. One former detective said jihadists were enrolling on university courses to collect the student loans "often with no intention of turning up".

But he probably accessed other types of benefits as well, particularly since he never worked and had plenty of cash.

…the Department for Work and Pensions refused to say if Abedi had received any benefits, including housing benefit and income support worth up to £250 a week, during 2015 and 2016.

…Abedi, 22, never held down a job, according to neighbours and friends, but was able to travel regularly between the UK and Libya. Abedi also had sufficient funds to buy materials for his sophisticated bomb while living in a rented house in south Manchester. Six weeks before the bombing Abedi rented a second property in a block of flats in Blackley eight miles from his home, paying £700 in cash. He had enough money to rent a third property in the centre of Manchester from where he set off with a backpack containing the bomb. Abedi also withdrew £250 in cash three days before the attack and transferred £2,500 to his younger brother Hashim in Libya.

Time for another example. Remember the piece of human garbage in London who mowed down some innocent people with his car before murdering a policeman?

Well, he also was subsidized by taxpayers.

Khalid Masood, the radical ISIS terrorist responsible for London's Westminster terror attack, did not have a job and was receiving government benefits before engaging in his attack. …Masood had a violent criminal history, including several knife attacks. ... Terrorists receiving government welfare is a common theme discovered in many post-terror attack investigations.

Seems like Abedi and Masood should have had their own episode of "Benefits Street."

There are also new reports on welfare-subsidized terror from continental Europe.

A story in *USA Today* offers a depressing summary.

> Governments across Europe have accidentally paid taxpayer-funded welfare benefits such as unemployment funds, disability pensions and housing allowances to Islamic State militants who have used the money to wage war in Iraq and Syria, authorities and terrorism experts say. Danish officials said this week that 29 citizens were given $100,000 in public pension benefits because they were considered too ill or disabled to work, and they then fled to Syria to fight for the radical group. ...Other countries that also have paid benefits to Islamic State fighters...It took eight months before welfare authorities cut off benefits paid to a Swedish national who had joined the terror group in its Syrian stronghold Raqqa. ... Authorities concluded that several of the plotters in the Brussels and Paris terror attacks that killed 162 people in 2015 and 2016 were partly financed by Belgium's social welfare system while they planned their atrocities. ...radical Islamic cleric Anjem Choudary, who was jailed for terrorist activities, urged followers to claim "jihadiseeker's allowance" — a reference to the nation's welfare system. His phrase echoes a manual released by the militant group in 2015. *How to Survive in the West: A Mujahid Guide* advises that "if you can claim extra benefits from a government, then do so."

By the way, I don't know whether to laugh or cry about the Belgian government's response.

Are they reducing the welfare state? Of course not.

But you'll be happy to know that imprisoned radicals lose access to the government teat.

> Philippe de Koster, director of Belgium's agency that fights money laundering and terrorism financing, said steps have since been taken to prevent that from happening again. For example, those convicted of terrorism can no longer receive benefits while in jail.

I've already written about welfare-subsidized terrorism in the Nordic nations.

Here's another story about developments in Scandinavia.

> The report examined hundreds of individuals who left to join extremist groups such as Islamic State (IS, formerly ISIS/ISIL) between 2013 and 2016. Commissioned at the request of the Financial Supervisory Authority, it has found that the majority was still receiving living allowance, child benefit, maintenance support and parental benefits while abroad, having other people handle their mail to make it look like they were still at home.

The problem seems especially acute in Sweden.

> Close to every person who left Sweden to fight for terror groups in the Middle East received welfare to support themselves abroad, according to a new government report. A study of 300 Swedish citizens who fought in Syria and Iraq between 2013 and 2016 shows jihadis are getting increasingly good at getting away with welfare fraud. The individuals often use a person in Sweden to handle paperwork and create the illusion that they're still in the country. …The most attractive option are government loans to study abroad. The loans are easy to get and thousands of dollars are paid out at once. …The Danish Security and Intelligence Service (PET) recently identified several cases of Danish citizens

receiving early pension because they were deemed too sick or disabled to work. They later left the country to fight for Islamic State while the payments continue to get deposited into their accounts. …PET has tried to cut off the benefits since 2014, but current legislation doesn't allow the payment agency to cut early pensions simply because the recipient is believed to be a terrorist.

Let's close with something that it either astounding or depressing, or actually both. All of the examples cited above are nations with bloated welfare states. Governments in all those countries consume more than 40 percent of economic output, and more than 50 percent of GDP in some cases.

Belgium is in that latter category, yet one official actually said that it was very difficult to fight terrorism "due to the small size of the Belgian government."

To me, this is a reminder that the natural incompetence of government becomes worse the bigger it gets.

P.S. Today's column mocks European government for welfare-subsidized terrorism, but American readers should be careful about throwing stones in glass houses.

The dirtbags who bombed the Boston Marathon were mooching off taxpayers.

And the U.S. refugee program includes automatic eligibility for handouts, making it, in part, a "terrorist-funding welfare scam."

P.P.S. I suppose a concluding caveat would be appropriate. I'm not making an argument that welfare causes terrorism. That almost would be as silly as the leftists who claim that terrorism is caused by inequality or climate change. Though I do wonder whether people who get government handouts feel a sense of self-loathing that leaves them vulnerable to jihadist ideology.

Minimum Wage Increases Are Bad News for Low-Skilled Workers in General, not Just for those Who Lose their Jobs

June 27, 2017

When I debate my leftist friends on the minimum wage, it's often a strange experience. When other people are listening or watching, they'll adopt a very extreme position and basically claim that politicians have the power to dramatically boost take-home pay by simply mandating higher levels of pay. And somehow there won't be any noticeable negative impact on employment and labor markets, even though businesses only create jobs if they expect some net profit.

But when we talk privately, they have a more nuanced argument. They'll confess that higher minimum wages will cause some low-skilled workers to become unemployed, but then justify that outcome using either or both of these arguments.

- Amoral utilitarianism – A large number of people will get pay raises and only a small handful will lose their jobs, and this is okay if policy is based on some notion of greatest good for the greatest number. In other words, you can't make an omelet without breaking a few eggs.

- Keynesian stimulus – Some people will lose their jobs, but the income gains for those who keep their jobs will boost "aggregate demand" and thus provide a boost for the economy. Sort of like they also claim giving people unemployment benefits will somehow generate more economic activity.

I've always rejected the first argument because I believe in the individual right of contract. The government should not prevent an employer and employee from engaging in voluntary exchange.

And I've always rejected the second argument because there can't be any net "stimulus" since any additional income for workers is automatically offset by less income for employers.

So who is right?

Well, the real world just kicked advocates of higher minimum wages in the teeth. Or maybe even someplace even more painful. A new study from the National Bureau of Economic Research looks at the impact of the $11 and $13 minimum wages in the city of Seattle and finds very bad results.

Let's start by simply citing what the local government did.

This paper, using rich administrative data on employment, earnings and hours in Washington State, re-examines this prediction in the context of Seattle's minimum wage increases from $9.47 to $11/hour in April 2015 and to $13/hour in January 2016.

And here's a table (following page) from the study, showing details on the minimum-wage mandate.

And what's been happening as a result of this intervention in the labor market?

Unsurprisingly, the jump to $13 has been much more damaging that the jump to $11.

> ...conclusion: employment losses associated with Seattle's mandated wage increases are in fact large enough to have resulted in net reductions in payroll expenses – and total employee earnings – in the low-wage job market. ...We show that the impact of Seattle's minimum wage increase on wage levels is much smaller than the statutory increase, reflecting the fact that most affected low-wage workers were already earning more than the statutory minimum at

baseline. Our estimates imply, then, that conventionally calculated elasticities are substantially underestimated. Our preferred estimates suggest that the rise from $9.47 to $11 produced disemployment effects that approximately offset wage effects, with elasticity estimates around -1. The subsequent increase to as much as $13 yielded more substantial disemployment effects, with net elasticity estimates closer to -3.

Table 1: Minimum Wage Schedule in Seattle under the Seattle Minimum Wage Ordinance

| Effective Date | Large Employers[a] | | Small Employers | |
	No benefits	With benefits[b]	No benefits or tips	Benefits or tips[c]
	Before Seattle Ordinance			
January 1, 2015	$9.47	$9.47	$9.47	$9.47
	After Ordinance			
April 1, 2015	$11.00	$11.00	$11.00	$10.00
January 1, 2016	$13.00	$12.50	$12.00	$10.50
January 1, 2017	$15.00[d]	$13.50	$13.00	$11.00
January 1, 2018		$15.00[e]	$14.00	$11.50
January 1, 2019			$15.00[f]	$12.00
January 1, 2020				$13.50
January 1, 2021				$15.00[g]

Here's a chart (see following page) from the study looking at the impact on hours worked.

If you want a healthy labor market, it's not good to be below the line.

And here's some of the explanatory text.

…Because the estimated magnitude of employment losses exceeds the magnitude of wage gains in the second phase-in period, we would expect a decline in total payroll for jobs paying under $13 per hour relative to baseline. Indeed, we observe this decline in first-differences when comparing "peak" calendar quarters, as shown in Table 3 above. …point estimates suggest payroll declines of 4.0% to 7.6% (averaging 5.8%) during the second phase-in period. This implies that the minimum wage increase to $13 from the baseline level of $9.47 reduced income paid to low-wage employees of single-location Seattle businesses by roughly $120 million on an annual basis. …Our preferred estimates suggest that the Seattle Minimum Wage Ordinance caused hours worked by low-skilled workers (i.e., those earning under $19 per hour) to fall by 9.4% during the three quarters when the minimum wage was $13 per hour, resulting in a loss of 3.5 million hours worked per calendar quarter. Alternative estimates show the number of low-wage jobs declined by 6.8%, which represents a loss of more than 5,000 jobs.

Appendix Figure 3: Estimated impact of the minimum wage on the quarterly hours worked in jobs paying <$19 per hour, all industries.

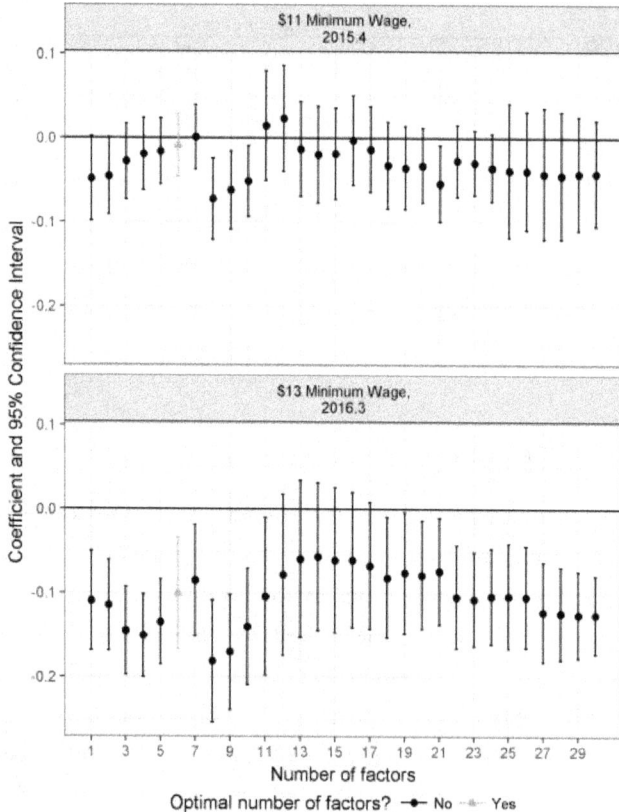

But the biggest takeaway from the report is that hours dropped so much that the average low-wage worker wound up with less income

> The reduction in hours would cost the average employee $179 per month, while the wage increase would recoup only $54 of this loss, leaving a net loss of $125 per month (6.6%), which is sizable for a low-wage worker.

Here's the relevant chart.

Once again, it's not good to be below the line.

Appendix Figure 4: Estimated impact of the minimum wage on the quarterly payroll to jobs paying <$19 per hour, all industries.

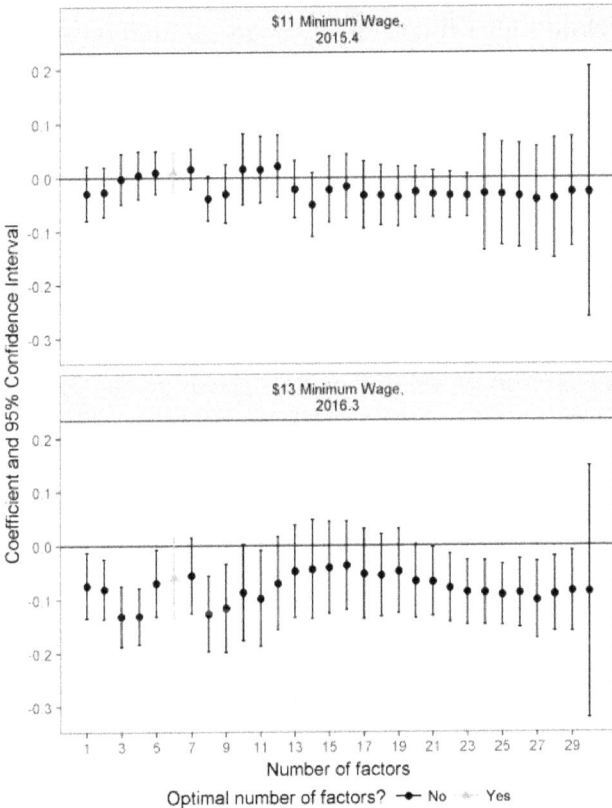

This data is remarkable because it shows that higher minimum wages are a bad idea, even according to the metrics of our friends on the left.

- The amoral utlitarianism argument doesn't apply because it's no longer possible to claim that income gains for those keeping jobs will more than offset income losses for those who become unemployed.

- The Keynesian aggregate-demand argument doesn't apply because it's no longer possible to assert macroeconomic benefits based on the assumption of a net increase in "spending power" in the economy.

Let's close with a couple of observations from others who have looked at the new study.

Diana Furchtgott-Roth of the Manhattan Institute (and formerly Chief Economist at the Department of Labor) highlights the most relevant findings.

> Raising the pay floor has led to net losses in payroll expenses and worker incomes for low-wage workers. ...When hourly wages rose from $11 to $13 in 2016, hours of work and earnings for low-wage workers were reduced by 9 percent for the first three calendar quarters, resulting in 3.5 million fewer hours worked for each calendar quarter. The number of jobs declined by 7 percent, with the result that 5,000 jobs were lost. ...The evidence shows that in Seattle, low-wage workers got less money in their pockets, rather than more.

Some proponents of intervention and mandates may want to dismiss Diana's analysis since of her reputation as a market-friendly scholar.

But even Ben Casselman and Kathryn Casteel of *FiveThirtyEight* basically reach the same conclusion.

As cities across the country pushed their minimum wages to untested heights in recent years, some economists began to ask: How high is too high? Seattle, with its highest-in-the-country minimum wage, may have hit that limit. …New research released Monday by a team of economists at the University of Washington suggests the wage hike may have come at a significant cost: The increase led to steep declines in employment for low-wage workers, and a drop in hours for those who kept their jobs. Crucially, the negative impact of lost jobs and hours more than offset the benefits of higher wages — on average, low-wage workers earned $125 per month *less* because of the higher wage.

I'm amused to find more evidence that left-leaning economists admit that higher minimum wages cause damage, albeit never on the record.

Even some liberal economists have expressed concern, often privately, that employers might respond differently to a minimum wage of $12 or $15, which would affect a far broader swath of workers.

I'm wondering how they can look at themselves in the mirror. It seems very immoral (in other words, beyond amoral) to publicly defend a policy that you privately admit is bad.

I understand that this type of dishonesty happens all the time in the political world (for example, some Republicans are now supporting Trump's plans for infrastructure boondoggles and parental leave when they would have been strongly opposed if the same policies had been proposed by Obama).

But what's the point of being a tenured academic if you can't at least be honest?

Though maybe there's some sort of cognitive dissonance at play, where they feel the rules of honesty don't apply in the political world. For instance, both Paul Krugman and Larry Summers have acknowledged in their academic work that unemployment benefits lead to more unemployment. But they pretend that's not the case when commenting on the policy debate.

But I'm digressing.

GENUINE FEDERALISM AND TAX COMPETITION FOR AUSTRALIA?

APRIL 3, 2016

Australia is one of my favorite nations, and not just because the people are friendly.

It has a modest-sized government, at least compared to other developed nations, and it has a very attractive private Social Security system that puts Australia in relatively good shape when looking at the long-run fiscal health of countries.

Indeed, this is one of the reasons why I picked Australia when asked which nation to choose if (when?) America suffers a Greek-style fiscal and economic collapse.

But this surely doesn't mean that Australia has ideal public policy. It ranks #11 for economic freedom, which is better than America, but the Aussies trail first-place Hong Kong by more than one full point in the 1-10 scoring system.

That being said, Australia will probably move in the right direction if Prime Minister Malcolm Turnbull succeeds in his plan to implement real federalism by shrinking the central government and returning tax and spending authority to the states.

Here's how an Australian media report characterized the issue.

> Returning income taxing power to the states would have resulted in a fierce interstate economic battle that would see Australians vote with their feet and move their lives across borders to get a better deal, economists warn.

The reporter obviously is talking to left-wing economists. If she talked to sensible economists, the above sentence would end with "hope" rather than "warn."

Here are some of the specific details.

> The Prime Minister met with state premiers and territory chief ministers yesterday to discuss his plan to lower the federal government's income tax and have the states make up the rest by collecting their own tax, to do with which whatever they please. If his bold scheme had gone ahead, they would eventually have been able to set their own tax rates as well.

Unfortunately, state-level politicians apparently are not happy with the notion of having real responsibility.

> ...premiers and chief ministers weren't keen and the idea is now off the table, for now, after Malcolm Turnbull conceded there was "nothing like a consensus".

Actually, there was a consensus of the state politicians. If you'll allow me to provide a negative interpretation, they want the empty-suit job of taking money from the nation's central government and then playing Santa Claus by distributing that money to various interest groups.

But I hope Turnbull isn't giving up because of resistance by these hacks.

Here are some more excerpts that help to explain why he has a very good idea.

> What he had been attempting to do with the tax shift was to force more responsibility onto state governments, and encourage greater accountability to its voters. It's a new way of funding school and hospitals and is also designed to encourage competition between the states and force them to operate more efficiently. It's a model

called competitive federalism, which allows states to battle it out over a range of issues to compete to provide their citizens with the best value goods and services at the best cost.

And the reporter did talk to at least one good economist, my buddy Sinclair Davidson.

RMIT economist Professor Sinclair Davidson explains…"At the moment, because the federal government has so much power over the revenue that goes into health and education, for example, there's not much difference between the states…But once that changes, for people whose state's bundles of goods and services don't suit their needs, they can start looking around." With a mobile population threatening to abandon its state government, effectively stripping it of a major revenue supply, the voting public would have a lot more control over state governments, Prof Davidson says. …With state governments made more eager to please, it sounds like this new tax plan would be a win for voters, if those downward pressures on tax rates the system's meant to encourage do come off.

Here's a different perspective.

Curtin University Associate Professor Helen Hodgson argues state tax competition could lead to a race to the bottom. "The biggest challenge that would emerge is if states chose to exercise the right to increase or decrease their income tax rates," she writes… Prof Hodgson says boosting migration between the states would put pressure on state governments to reduce their own rates as they compete to retain their populations, while "a general lowering of tax rates would defeat the stated intention of allowing states to raise additional funding for health and education."

Methinks Professor Hodgson's "stated intention" is not the same as Prime Minister Turnbull's "stated intention."

Here's some more analysis from a column in *The Conversation*.

> Malcolm Turnbull has called for a dramatic shift in Australia's model of federalism... Many economists regard this as sensible and much-overdue reform...the argument is for a shift from a federal income tax to a state income tax. In principle, this can be done in a completely revenue-neutral way. ...that would, on the whole, benefit Australian taxpayers because a more efficient tax system is a less costly tax system.

But it wouldn't benefit state politicians in Australia. With the exception of Western Australia's Colin Barnett, they don't like accountability and responsibility.

> state premiers...hated the idea. It's important to understand why. This is not because the idea is bad for the citizens of the states, with the premiers being outraged on their behalf. Rather it is because it is bad for the political classes themselves, and the premiers in particular.

Citing the groundbreaking work of economist Charles Tiebout, the article includes a description of why tax competition between sub-national governments is desirable.

> The basic idea is that the states compete with each other by offering bundles of public goods at different prices (i.e. taxes). This is the significance of the state-level income tax. Victoria, for example, may offer very high levels of public services, but also at a high price through high state income taxes. NSW may offer more moderate public services, but also much lighter taxes. What happens next is that citizens sort themselves over the states according to their preferences. Those who value high levels of public services move to Victoria, where they pay that marginal valuation in high taxes. Citizens with preferences for lower levels of public services and also taxes move to NSW. This is a market,

not a political, model of local public goods. Economists like it because it encourages competition between the states to provide an efficient bundle of public goods and services at a point that voters (as consumers) are willing to pay. This competition tends to produce an efficient outcome.

Here's the bottom line. The current system creates a perverse incentive for state officials to endlessly whine for more money. Putting state governments in charge creates an appropriate balance of responsibility and accountability.

> That is not the situation we have now. Premiers are incentivised to represent their citizens as all wanting the maximum amount of public goods and services, because someone else is paying for them. State income taxes (coupled with reduced federal income taxes) are a way of implementing this mechanism. The main winners from this will be the 7 million or so Australian taxpayers, because it will deliver a much more efficient supply of public goods and services. The main losers will be the state and territory premiers, because they will have to compete in the market for political goods and services.

Heaven forbid, politicians actually having to collect and spend their own money. Especially in a system where taxpayers can look across state borders to see which states are doing a bad job or good job (think Texas vs. California). How cruel that would be! They would be forced…gasp…to compete.

But let's set aside sarcasm. It's worth noting that the most decentralized major economy is Switzerland, and that system has worked quite well.

And the United States also compares favorably with other developed nations, even though we've allowed Washington to grab powers that more properly belong at the state level (or in the private sector).

Hopefully, Turnbull's plan in Australia will move forward and create additional evidence that America should return to the more robust federalist system that our Founders envisioned.

New Zealand's Road Map for Sweeping Pro-Market Reform

August 9, 2017

I wrote last September that New Zealand is the unsung success story of the world.

No, it doesn't rank above Hong Kong and Singapore, which routinely rank as the two jurisdictions with the most economic liberty.

But it deserves praise for rising so far and fast considering how the country was mired in statist misery just three decades ago. That's the story of this great video, narrated by Johan Norberg, from Free to Choose Media. It's runs 56 minutes, but it's very much worth your time.

But just in case you don't have a spare hour to watch the full video, I can tell you that it explains how New Zealand made a radical shift to free markets in key areas such as agriculture, trade, fisheries, and industry.

I wrote about New Zealand's shift to a property rights-based fisheries system, which is a remarkable success. But I'm even more impressed that the country, which has a very significant agricultural sector, decided to eliminate all subsidies. I fantasize about similar reforms in the United States.

To give you an idea of New Zealand's overall deregulatory success, it is now ranked first in the World Bank's *Doing Business*.

As a fiscal policy wonk, my one complaint is that the video doesn't give much attention to tax and budget policy.

Which is an unfortunate oversight because there's a very positive story to tell. In the early 1990s, the government basically imposed a nominal spending freeze. And during that five-year period, the burden of government spending fell by more than 10-percentage points of GDP.

And because policy makers dealt with the underlying disease of too much spending, that also meant eliminating the symptom of red ink. In other words, a big deficit became a big surplus.

The same thing also has been happening this decade. Outlays have been increasing by an average of less than 2 percent annually. And because this complies with my Golden Rule, that means a shrinking burden of spending.

And there's also a good story to tell about tax policy. The top income tax rate has been slashed from 66 percent to 33 percent, and the capital gains tax has been abolished.

Let's close by highlighting what should be the main lesson of the video, namely that any country can rescue itself from economic decline.

As I watched, the first thing that occurred to me is that New Zealand's reforms are – or at least should be – a road map for Greece to follow.

The Fraser Institute's *Economic Freedom of the World* shows the history of economic liberty in the two nations, and you can see that they used to be very similar – in a bad way – back in the 1970s. They began to diverge between 1975 and 1985, mostly because policy got even worse in Greece. Then both adopted better policy started in 1985, but New Zealand went much farther in the right direction.

Policy has been generally stable in both nations this century. That's acceptable for New Zealand, but it's basically a recipe for continued misery in Greece.

But the good news is that Greece can simply copy New Zealand to get the same good results.

P.S. Remember when Gary Johnson caught grief for being unable to list any admirable foreign leaders. I defended him by pointing out that there are not any obvious choices in office today, but I did mention that Roger Douglas and Ruth Richardson would be on list if it included former politicians.

P.P.S. New Zealand ranks #3 for total human freedom, trailing only Hong Kong and Switzerland.

TWO REASONS WHY POLICY STABILITY MEANS ECONOMIC DECLINE FOR ITALY

JULY 22, 2017

I'm rather pessimistic about Italy.

Simply stated, it's economy is moribund. If you peruse the OECD's economic database, you'll see that both inflation-adjusted GDP and inflation-adjusted private consumption expenditure (in some ways a more accurate measure of actual quality of life) have grown by an average of just slightly over one percent annually this century.

And even though Italy's population growth has been anemic, there are more people. And when you add a larger population to the equation, you get per-capita changes in output and living standards that are even less impressive.

But not everyone shares my dour outlook. I recently exchanged views with someone who said that Italy hasn't increased the burden of government in recent years.

And that person is right. Sort of.

Here's a chart showing Italy's score from *Economic Freedom of the World* since the start of the 21st century. As you can see with the chart on the following page, it's been remarkably stable.

Economic Freedom Score by Year(s) - World Ranking

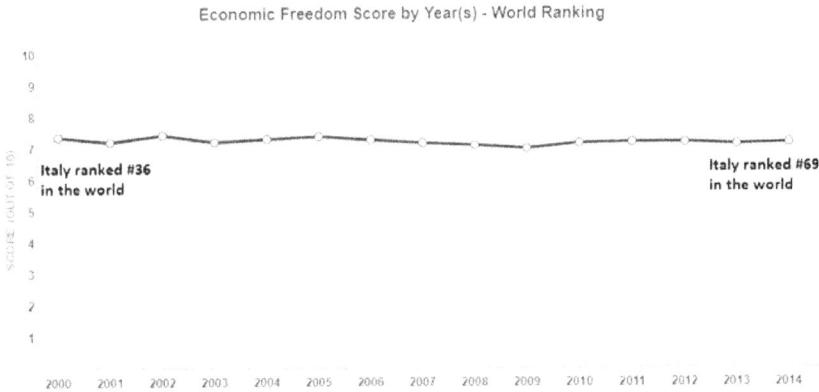

But I have two reasons why I think policy stability is a recipe for economic decline.

First, you don't win a race by standing still if others are moving forward. If you look closely at the above chart, you will see that Italy used to be ranked #36 in the world for economic freedom but it now ranks #69. In other words, Italy's absolute level of economic freedom barely changed over the period, but its relative position declined significantly because other nations engaged in reforms and leapfrogged Italy in the rankings.

Second, Italy is in the middle of dramatic demographic changes that will have a huge impact on fiscal policy. People are living longer and having fewer children, but Italy's welfare state was set up on the assumption that there would be lots of working-age taxpayers to finance old-age beneficiaries. In other words, policy stability will lead to fiscal crisis thanks to changes in the composition of the population. Think Greece, but on a bigger scale.

And when I refer to Greece on a bigger scale, I'm thinking another fiscal crisis.

Demond Lachman of the American Enterprise Institute is

pessimistic about Italy and warns that high levels of red ink could cause a big mess.

> We've got an Italian economy that is categorized by extremely high public debt. Their public debt level is now something like 132% of GDP, they've got a banking system that is bust, that banks have something like 18% of their loans non-performing, that is a huge amount, the economy is completely sclerotic, that the level of Italian GDP today is pretty much the same as it was some fifteen years ago. There's been practically no growth, declining living standards... What also makes Italy very important from a global point of view is that we're now not talking about a small country like Greece which doesn't have that much systemic significance. We're talking about the third largest country in the Eurozone. We're talking about a country that has the world's third largest sovereign bond market with something like two and a half trillion dollars of debt.

And don't forget that these grim fiscal numbers probably mean even higher taxes on Italy's young workers.

But those taxpayers aren't captives. Cristina Odone, in a column for CapX, points out that young people are getting the short end of the stick.

> Gerontocracy, stifling regulations and huge unemployment have hindered Italy's prosperity for decades now. The country hailed for its economic miracle and famed for its creative and industrious entrepreneurs (at the helm, usually, of family-run businesses such as Gucci, Prada, and Ferrero) today comes second only to Greece (among EU countries) for the size of its national debt. ...Italy's unemployed youngsters, who constitute 40 per cent of under-24-year-olds, gnash their teeth at the unfairness of national life, where fossils control the levers of power while flouting their sinecures. A quarter of under-30-year-olds classify as NEETS,

young people who are not in education, work or training. Contrast this with the UK, where only one in 10 under the age of 30 is in the same position. …Labour laws continue to blight young people's prospects. …This sclerosis risks turning Italy into the sick man of Europe.

No wonder many young Italians are migrating to nations with more economic opportunity. *AFP* has a story on the dour outlook in Italy.

With the country struggling to kick an economic slump, some 40,000 Italians between 18 and 34 years old set out to seek greener pastures elsewhere in 2015, according to the Migrantes Foundation. "Just talking with people (in Italy) it's clear going away might be the only solution," said D'Elia, 26, who has spent the last five years in London, where he currently works as a barman, and intends to stay for now despite high living costs. …most of Italy's youths are unwilling to return — and the country is seen as offering little to attract foreign graduates. …GDP is forecast to inch up just 1.3 percent this year. The jobless rate hovers at over 11 percent, well above the euro area average of 9.3 percent. Among 15 to 24-year olds it leaps to 37 percent, compared with a European average of 18.7 percent. …Sergio Mello, who set up a start-up in Hong Kong before moving to San Francisco, said Italy "does not offer a fertile environment to develop a competitive business". …Mello says there are other problems: "The bureaucracy wastes a lot of time", the red tape "drives you crazy".

Unfortunately, rather than ease up on government burdens so that young people will have some hope for the future, some Italian politicians want new mandates, new spending, new taxes, and new restrictions.

I've previously written about new destructive tax policies that shrink the tax base. And I've written about wasteful new spending schemes, like a €500 "culture bonus."

And now there's something equally silly on the regulatory front being proposed by politicians. Here are excerpts from a report by *Heat Street* on the initiative.

> Italy could soon become the first Western country to offer paid "menstrual leave" to female workers. …If passed, it would mandate that companies enforce a "menstrual leave" policy and offer three paid days off each month to working women who experience painful periods. …The Italian version of *Marie Claire* described it as "a standard-bearer of progress and social sustainability." But the bill also has critics, including women who fear this sort of measure could backfire and end up stigmatizing them. Writing in Donna Moderna, another women's magazine, Lorenza Pleuteri argued that if women were granted extra paid leave, employers would be even more reluctant to hire women, in a country where women already struggle to integrate the workforce. …Miriam Goi, a feminist writer, …fears that rather than breaking taboos about women's menstrual cycle, the measure could end up perpetuating the idea that women are more emotional than men and require special treatment.

It's unclear if this policy was actually enacted, but it's a bad sign that it was even considered. Simply stated, making workers more expensive is not a good way to encourage more job creation. Even a columnist for the *New York Times* acknowledged that feminist-driven economic policies backfire against women.

The bottom line is that Italy needs sweeping reductions in the burden of the public sector. Yet the nation's politicians are more interested in expanding the size and scope of government. Perhaps now it's easy to understand why I fear the country may have passed the tipping point. You can be in a downward spiral even if policy doesn't change.

The New York Times (Accidentally) Debunks the Never-Ending Fairy Tale of Gun Control

Number 30, 2016

When I write about gun control, I generally make two arguments.

First, criminals are lawbreakers, so the notion that they will be disarmed because of gun control is a fantasy. Crooks and thugs who really want a gun will always have access to black-market weapons.

Second, to the extent that good people obey bad gun-control laws (and hopefully they won't), that will encourage more criminal activity since bad people will be less worried about armed resistance.

These points are common sense, but they doesn't seem to convince many leftists, who have a religious-type faith that good intentions will produce good results (they need to read Bastiat!).

Every so often, however, the other side accidentally messes up.

As part of its never-ending, ideologically driven campaign to undermine gun rights, the *New York Times* ran a big 5,000-plus word story last month about mass shootings. Creating hostility to guns was the obvious goal of this "news" report.

But buried in all that verbiage was a remarkable admission. A big majority of shooters already are in violation of gun laws.

> The New York Times examined all 130 shootings last year in
> which four or more people were shot, at least one fatally, and

> investigators identified at least one attacker. …64 percent of the shootings involved at least one attacker who violated an existing gun law.

And for the 36 percent of the nutjobs in the story who purchased or obtained guns legally, almost all of them presumably would have gotten their hands on weapons even if they had to violate minor laws on guns prior to violating major laws against murder.

So what the New York Times and other anti-second amendment activists are really saying is that honest people should be defenseless even though bad guys always will have the ability to arm themselves. And by making such a preposterous claim, they actually provided ammo (pun intended) for those of us who defend the Second Amendment.

P.S. Maybe we should give the *New York Times* a "Wrong-Way Corrigan Award" for inadvertently helping to make the libertarian case for more freedom! Oh, and give Trevor Noah the Award at the same time.

P.P.S. Years ago, I used to post lots of gun-control humor. I've gotten out of the habit, but I can't resist sharing some items that popped into my inbox yesterday.

The first one is one of my favorites.

The second one brought back fond childhood memories. Somehow I avoided becoming a killer even though I grew up watching Yosemite Sam, Elmer Fudd, and other trigger-happy angry white men. Not to mention shows like Combat and Rat Patrol!

Last but not least, the third and final one reminds me that crazed mass shooters are always sufficiently un-crazy that they manage to pick out gun-free zones before engaging in their rampages.

So maybe, just maybe, the problem isn't guns. Indeed, perhaps we can draw the conclusion that society will be safer if more good people are armed.

Heck, even big-city police chiefs are beginning to reach that conclusions.

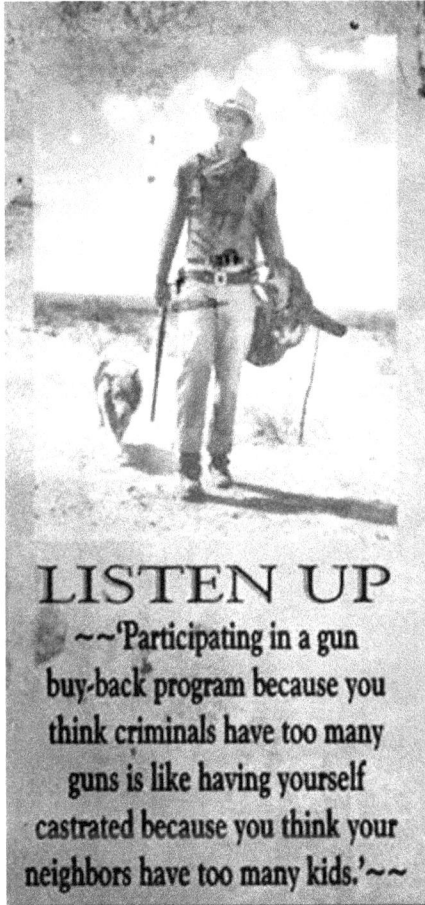

LISTEN UP
~~'Participating in a gun buy-back program because you think criminals have too many guns is like having yourself castrated because you think your neighbors have too many kids.'~~

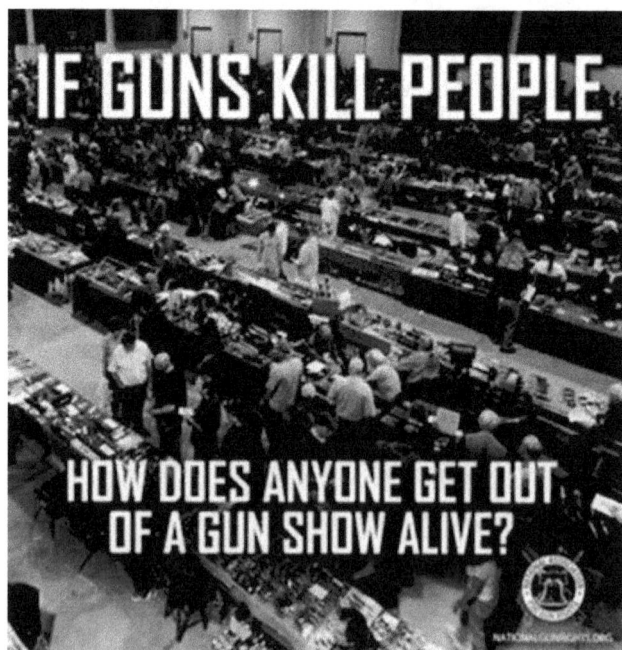

VENEZUELA'S ACCELERATING DESCENT TO SOCIALIST MISERY

MAY 18, 2017

Nations usually don't suffer overnight economic collapse. Indeed, Adam Smith was right about the ability of a country to survive and withstand lots of bad public policy.

But at some point, as a nation gravitates in the wrong direction on the statism spectrum, it goes from prosperity to stagnation to decline.

Which is sort of what happened in Argentina because of Peronism (though Pope Francis learned the wrong lesson from his country's big mistake).

But Venezuela is even worse. It's going from prosperity to stagnation to decline to collapse.

In a must-read article for the Mises Institute, José Niño explains how cronyism and redistributionism helped to sap Venezuela's economy way before Chavez and Maduro made a bad situation far worse.

> While Chávez and his successor Nicolás Maduro deserve the brunt of the blame for Venezuela's current economic calamity, the underlying flaws of Venezuela's political economy point to much more systemic problems. …Years of gradual economic interventionism took what was once a country bound to join the ranks of the First World to a middle-tier developing country.

This steady decline eventually created an environment where a demagogue like Chávez would completely exploit for his political gain.

But it wasn't always this way. Indeed, Venezuela at one point was market-oriented and prosperous.

From the 1910s to the 1930s, the much-maligned dictator Juan Vicente Gómez...modernized an otherwise neocolonial backwater by allowing market actors, domestic and foreign, to freely exploit newly discovered oil deposits. Venezuela would experience substantial economic growth and quickly establish itself as one of Latin America's most prosperous countries by the 1950s. In the 1950s, General Marcos Pérez Jiménez would continue Gómez's legacy. At this juncture, Venezuela was at its peak, with a fourth place ranking in terms of per capita GDP worldwide. ...A combination of a relatively free economy, an immigration system that attracted and assimilated laborers from Italy, Portugal, and Spain, and a system of strong property rights, allowed Venezuela to experience unprecedented levels of economic development from the 1940s up until the 1970s.

But the seeds of economic decline were planted during this time.

Pérez Jiménez did introduce some elements of crony capitalism, pharaonic public works projects, and increased state involvement in "strategic industries" like the steel industry. ...social democrat political leader Rómulo Betancourt would...assume the presidency from 1959 to 1964. The Fourth Republic of Venezuela — Venezuela's longest lasting period of democratic rule, was established... Venezuela's Fourth Republic marked the beginning of a process of creeping socialism that gradually whittled away at Venezuela's economic and institutional foundations. ...Betancourt still believed in a very activist role for the State in economic matters. Betancourt was part of a generation of intellectuals and student activists that aimed to fully nationalize Venezuela's petroleum sector and use petroleum rents to establish a welfare state... At its core, this vision of economic organization assumed that the government must manage the economy through central planning.

And policy went further left in the 1970s. And beyond.

In 1975, ...Carlos Andrés Pérez's government nationalized the petroleum sector. The nationalization of Venezuela's oil industry fundamentally altered the nature of the Venezuelan state. Venezuela morphed into a petrostate, in which the concept of the consent of the governed was effectively turned on its head. Instead of Venezuelans paying taxes to the government in exchange for the protection of property and similar freedoms, the Venezuelan state would play a patrimonial role by bribing its citizens with all sorts of handouts to maintain its dominion over them. ...Pérez would take advantage of this state power-grab to finance a profligate welfare state and a cornucopia of social welfare programs... Venezuela's economy became overwhelmingly politicized. ...the nationalization of the petroleum industry...laid the groundwork for institutional decay that would clearly manifest itself during the 80s and 90s.

Jose's article is a valuable contribution to the discussion.

Indeed, if you peruse the historical data at *Economic Freedom of the World*, you'll find that Venezuela enjoyed a high degree of economic freedom at late as the early 1970s.

And it's no coincidence that Venezuela was much richer than its neighbors at the time. But bad policy has caused economic decline, and bad policy has accelerated as the country has shifted from cronyism and vote buying to explicit socialism (otherwise known as entering the fourth circle of statist hell).

Let's look at what big government has produced in Venezuela.

An article in *Foreign Policy* sees parallels in the collapse of the Soviet Union and the disintegration of Venezuela.

> Venezuela is not the first developed country to put itself on track to fall into a catastrophic economic crisis. But it is in the relatively unusual situation of having done so while in possession of enormous oil assets. ...the Soviet Union's similar devastation in the late 1980s...may be instructive for Venezuela... The Venezuelan government, though it doesn't claim to be full-fledged in its devotion to Marxism-Leninism, has been pursuing as absurd an economic policy mix as its Soviet predecessor. It has insisted for years on maintaining drastic price controls... the government financed the budget deficit by printing money. The inevitable result was skyrocketing inflation. ...The collapse of the Maduro regime will not be pretty, but it is difficult to see how it can be avoided.

Hopefully, the collapse will happen quickly.

A thoroughly depressing story in the Wall Street Journal reveals the suffering of the country's poor people.

> Jean Pierre Planchart, a year old, has...a cry that is little more than a whimper. His ribs show through his skin. He weighs just 11 pounds. His mother, Maria Planchart, tried to feed him what she could find combing through the trash—scraps of chicken or potato. She finally took him to a hospital in Caracas, where she prays a rice-milk concoction keeps her son alive. ...Her country was once Latin America's richest, producing food for export. Venezuela now can't grow enough to feed its own people in an economy hobbled by the nationalization of private farms, and price and currency controls. ...Venezuela has the world's highest inflation—estimated by the International Monetary Fund to reach 720% this year—making it nearly impossible for families to make ends meet. Since 2013, the economy has shrunk 27%... Hordes of

people, many with children in tow, rummage through garbage… People in the countryside pick farms clean at night, stealing everything from fruits hanging on trees to pumpkins on the ground, adding to the misery of farmers hurt by shortages of seed and fertilizer. Looters target food stores. Families padlock their refrigerators. …Dr. Machado and her team of doctors are seeing a dramatic increase in emaciated infants brought to the Domingo Luciani Hospital in Caracas, where they work. …The most recent Caritas study of 800 children under the age of 5 in Yare and three other communities showed that in February nearly 11% suffered from severe acute malnutrition, which is potentially fatal…nearly a fifth of children under age 5 in those four communities suffered from chronic malnutrition. …Nearly a third of Venezuelans, 9.6 million people, eat two or fewer meals a day…four of out five in the nation are now poor.

But not everyone is suffering, reports the U.K.-based Times.

Ministers in President Maduro's government have been accused of hypocrisy by Venezuelans struggling to feed themselves after it emerged that many children and cronies of senior officials are living abroad in luxury. …The scandal has been likened to that of the "princelings" in China — the sons and daughters of Communist Party officials who have been exposed as leading lavish capitalist lifestyles. The recent series of outings of the children of Maduro's inner circle began with the case of Lucía Rodríguez, daughter of Jorge Rodríguez, the hard-left mayor of Caracas, and niece of Delcy Rodríguez, the foreign minister. Both politicians routinely describe the opposition in Venezuela as the "bourgeoisie". After Ms Rodríguez began posting images of her own bourgeois life in Sydney, where she is enrolled in a media studies course at the private SAE university, she was tracked down by an opposition activist to Bondi Beach, where she was photographed surfing and sipping cocktails. ...Rumours have long surrounded the suspiciously lavish lifestyles of two of the daughters of Mr Maduro's predecessor and mentor, Hugo Chávez. María Gabriela Chávez, the late president's elder daughter, is the deputy ambassador to the United Nations. Opposition MPs claim that she is a billionaire. She has been likened to the socialite Paris Hilton... Many families linked to the Maduro government and former officials have moved to America, despite it being denounced as the evil "imperio" by the president.

While the socialist elite enjoy luxury, unimaginable misery spreads across Venezuela.

Thousands of babies died in Venezuela last year, new official data show, highlighting the tragic impact of the country's economic crisis... The health ministry said deaths of infants under the age of one soared by 30 percent in 2016, a year when hospitals and protesters complained of severe shortages of medical supplies. Deaths of mothers linked to childbirth soared by two-thirds meanwhile, according to the data published by the ministry — the latest such figures since 2015. ...The Venezuelan Medical Federation says hospitals have only three percent of the medicines and supplies that they need to operate normally.

Given these horrifying and outrageous stories, is anyone surprised that this is happening?

There has been violence and widespread looting this week in Valencia, a once bustling industrial hub two hours from the capital by road. In an incident loaded with symbolism, a group of young men destroyed a statue of the late leader Hugo Chávez... Footage shows the statue, which depicts Chávez saluting and wearing a sash, being yanked down to cheers in a public plaza before it is bashed into a sidewalk and then the road as onlookers swear at the leftist, who died in 2013… "Students destroyed this statue of Chávez. They accuse him, correctly, of destroying their future," the opposition lawmaker Carlos Valero said about the incident… Venezuela's opposition…now enjoys majority support… Polls show the ruling Socialists would badly lose any conventional vote due to four years of economic crisis that has led to debilitating food and medicine shortages.

Or this?

Eugenio Vásquez Orellana, who was former Venezuelan President Hugo Chavez's minister of public banking, probably shouldn't have gone to a Venezuelan bakery in Miami, Florida. Shouts of "thief" and "rat" rang out as the crowd realized who this man was.

He should be grateful that he wasn't tarred and feathered. Or worse.

Let's review some additional examples of Venezuela's misery.

The *Wall Street Journal* reports on the plight of low-level government security officials.

Ana, a five-year veteran of the national police, …and her colleagues use tear gas and rubber bullets against increasingly desperate protesters armed with stones, Molotov cocktails and even bags of feces. The showdowns take place in scorching heat, and she says the authorities provide her with no food, water or overtime pay. … She and many of her exhausted colleagues say they are wavering as protests enter a seventh week with no end in sight. "One day I will step aside and just walk away, blend into the city," she said. "No average officers support this government anymore." …loyalty… has largely given way to demoralization, exhaustion and apathy amid an economic collapse and endless protests, said eight security officers from different forces and locations… Most of them say they want only to earn a steady wage amid crippling food shortages and a decimated private sector. Others say fear of a court-martial keeps them in line.

While I feel some empathy for poorly paid cops, who are doing bad things but mostly trying to keep their jobs, I have zero sympathy for these elites who merely want to wind up on the winning side.

…as Venezuela sinks into chaos, with clashes between protesters and the police escalating, why have its powerful political and military elites stuck by President Nicolás Maduro? … Demonstrators have overwhelmed city streets, so far undeterred by a police crackdown in which hundreds have been arrested and dozens killed. The violence deepens a monthslong crisis marked by food shortages, economic collapse and Mr. Maduro's fumbling attempts to consolidate authority. In quasi-democratic systems like Venezuela's, such pressures have often led elites to force a change, and have provided them an excuse to do so. …splits are beginning to emerge, as a few figures in major institutions signal opposition to Mr. Maduro, hinting at growing dissatisfaction and the government's inability to silence it. Recent actions by both elites and the government suggest they take the possibility of fracture seriously — maneuvering in a high-stakes contest… Elite fracture operates as a kind of game… Stay loyal to a failing government too long and you risk going down with it. But if you break with the government and others don't, you'll pay a high price for disloyalty. …Mr. Maduro can also play this game. He has enabled loyalists to profit from corruption and patronage, giving them a financial stake in the government's survival. …Drug and food smuggling also generate revenue, including for the military. But as the economy worsens, elites compete over a smaller pie. "When elites begin to compete among themselves, usually somebody defects," Mr. Levitsky said

Which suggests – fingers crossed – that the regime may soon collapse.

> In our 2017 forecast, we predicted that Venezuela's government would not survive the year. ...nationwide protests that seemed to be reaching a critical point, and the problem has not subsided. For more than a month now, large-scale protests against the government have taken place across the country nearly every day. The death toll continues to rise as protests show no sign of stopping. ... foreign intervention either in support of the government or of the opposition is not a viable way to end this crisis. ...International organizations could also intervene, but they lack the capability or political will to do so. ...Without foreign support, the opposition will need to rely heavily on public protests to increase pressure on the Maduro government. ...So far, Maduro has resisted resignation and a negotiated exit from power, believing he can withstand the protests against him. ...If the military and other security forces can no longer keep the protests in check, it will be a game changer for the Maduro government.

Shifting from news reports to opinion journalism, Kevin Williamson of *National Review* shares his thoughts.

> People are starving in Venezuela. That, too, is familiar enough to students of the history of socialism. The Ukrainian language contains a neologism—holodomor—necessitated by the fact that the socialist rulers of that country used agricultural policy to murder by starvation between 2 million and 5 million people who were guilty of the crime of resisting the socialists' agricultural policy. In the 1990s, famine killed something on the order of 10 percent of the population of North Korea, where people were reduced to cannibalism. A recent study found that the average Venezuelan has lost nearly 20 pounds in the past year as food supplies dwindle. ...Hayek and his colleagues in what has become known

as the Austrian school of economics, …believed that the central-planning aspirations of the socialists were not simply inefficient or unworkable but impossible to execute, even in principle… Hayek believed that efforts to impose central planning on economies were doomed to fail, and that this failure would not be met with humility but with outrage. …which leads to outright political repression, scapegoating, and violence. …there is something about socialism itself that throws up monsters.

Having endured all these depressing snippets of information (as well as the 28 horrifying headlines I shared last month), your reward is some dark humor.

In a video for *Reason*, Remy promotes the highly successful Venezuela Diet.

Let's close with a different type of humor.

It's time to mock the leftists who went on record in favor of Venezuela's totalitarian regime.

Recent figures show that a majority of Venezuelans go to bed hungry and 15 percent of people eat garbage to survive. The country desperately lacks basic resources, such as medicine and power. …Venezuela's problems date back to 1999, with the election of socialist president Hugo Chávez, whose mass redistribution of wealth and financial mismanagement laid the groundwork for the country's economic collapse. …Chávez's regime received plaudits from numerous left-wing academics, politicians, and celebrities who have now gone quiet.

Here are a few examples.

- The darling of the left, retired MIT professor Noam Chomsky was a supporter of Chávez's Venezuela and his anti-Americanism, arguing that he brought forward the "historic liberation of Latin America" proving "destructive to the rich oligarchy."

- Actor Sean Penn met with Hugo Chavez on numerous occasions, describing him as a "fascinating guy" who did "incredible things for the 80% of the people that are very poor there."

Film director Oliver Stone was such a fan of Chávez and the rise Latin American socialism that he made a film about it, entitled *South of the Border.* In the film, he conducted interviews with the continent's left-wing leaders, including Chávez, Cuba's Raúl Castro, Argentina's Cristina Fernández de Kirchner, and Bolivia's Evo Morales.

Civil rights activist Jesse Jackson…said there was no evidence that Venezuela posed a threat to the United States, while praising Chávez for his "focus on foreign debt, debt relief, and free and fair trade to overcome years of structural disorder, unnecessary military spending, [and] land reform." After Chávez's death, Jackson also offered a prayer at his funeral while celebrating his socialist legacy.

…filmmaker Michael Moore…, after Chávez's death, …praised him for "eliminating 75 percent of extreme poverty" while "[providing] free health and education for all."

The leader of the British Labour Party Jeremy Corbyn, …thanked Chávez for allegedly insuring "that the poor matter and wealth can be shared," adding he had made "massive contributions to Venezuela and the world."

The economist Joseph Stiglitz, a recipient of a Nobel Laureate, praised Hugo Chávez's socialist policies whilst on a visit to Caracas in 2007. Speaking at a World Economic Forum, Stiglitz said: "Venezuelan President Hugo Chavez appears to have had success in bringing health and education to the people in the poor neighbourhoods of Caracas."

And speaking of cosseted left-wing elites, does anyone think Bernie Sanders feels remorse for his support of Venezuela's evil government? If this interview is any indication, the answer is no.

THE ECONOMIC MISERY OF CUBAN COMMUNISM

SEPTEMBER 4, 2016

Communism should be remembered first and foremost for the death, brutality, and repression that occurred whenever that evil system was imposed upon a nation.

Dictators like Stalin, Mao, Pol Pot, the North Korean Kim dynasty either killed more than Hitler, or butchered higher proportions of their populations.

But let's not forget that communism also has an awful economic legacy. The economic breakdown of the Soviet Empire. The horrid deprivation in North Korea. The giant gap that existed between West Germany and East Germany. The mass poverty in China before partial liberalization.

Today, let's focus on how communism has severely crippled the Cuban economy.

In a column for *Reason* a few years ago, Steven Chapman accurately summarized the problems in that long-suffering nation.

> There may yet be admirers of Cuban communism in certain precincts of Berkeley or Cambridge, but it's hard to find them in Havana. ...the average Cuban makes only about $20 a month— which is a bit spartan even if you add in free housing, food, and medical care. For that matter, the free stuff is not so easy to come by: Food shortages are frequent, the stock of adequate housing has shrunk, and hospital patients often have to bring their own sheets,

food, and even medical supplies. ...Roger Noriega, a researcher at the conservative American Enterprise Institute in Washington, notes that before communism arrived, Cuba "was one of the most prosperous and egalitarian societies of the Americas." His colleague Nicholas Eberstadt has documented that pre-Castro Cuba had a high rate of literacy and a life expectancy surpassing that in Spain, Greece, and Portugal. Instead of accelerating development, Castro has hindered it. In 1980, living standards in Chile were double those in Cuba. Thanks to bold free-market reforms implemented in Chile but not Cuba, the average Chilean's income now appears to be four times higher than the average Cuban's. ...In its latest annual report, Human Rights Watch says, "Cuba remains the one country in Latin America that represses virtually all forms of political dissent."

The comparison between Chile and Cuba is especially apt since the pro-market reforms in the South American nation came after a coup against a Marxist government that severely weakened the Chilean economy.

Chapman points out that the standard leftist excuse for Cuban misery – the U.S. trade embargo – isn't very legitimate.

The regime prefers to blame any problems on the Yankee imperialists, who have enforced an economic embargo for decades. In fact, its effect on the Cuban economy is modest, since Cuba trades freely with the rest of the world.

Since the U.S. accounts for nearly one-fourth of world economic output, I'm open to the hypothesis that the negative impact on Cuba is more than "modest."

But it still would be just a partial explanation. Just remember that communist societies have always been economic basket cases even if they have unfettered ability to trade with all other nations.

Writing for the *Huffington Post* (hardly a pro-capitalism outfit), Terry Savage also explains that Cuba is an economic disaster.

> ...the economic consequences of a 50-year, totalitarian, socialistic experiment in government are obvious today. Cuba is a beautiful country filled with many friendly people, who have lived in poverty and deprivation for decades. Socialism in its purest form simply didn't work there. I was immediately reminded of that old saying: *"Capitalism is the unequal distribution of wealth – but socialism is the equal distribution of poverty."* Once-magnificent buildings are literally crumbling, plaster falling and walls and stairways falling apart, as there are no ownership incentives to maintain them – or profit potential to incent their preservation. ...Every Cuban gets a ration book and an assigned "bodega" in which to purchase the low-cost, subsidized food. The one I visited looked like an empty warehouse, with little on the shelves. If the rice, beans, eggs, and cooking oil are not in stock, the shopper must return the following week. Allowed five eggs per month, the basics barely cover a starvation existence. ...the economic results of their 50-year rule have been abysmal. Cuba became a protectorate of the old Soviet Union (remember the Cuban missile crisis) -and that worked until the early 1990s, when the USSR fell apart. No longer receiving aid from its protector, Cuba entered a long period now remembered as "the special times" – when Cubans were literally starving, when there was electricity only two hours per day, and people turned any patch of dirt into a garden to survive. Cubans bear the scars of that terrible time, and for many the current situation is still not that much better.

So Cuba was a basket case that was subsidized by the Soviet Union. When the Evil Empire collapsed and the subsidies ended, the basket case became a hellhole.

The good news, if we're grading on a curve, is that Cuba has now improved to again being a basket case.

But that improvement still leaves Cuba with a lot of room for improvement. It may not be at the level of North Korea, but it's worse than Venezuela, and that's saying something.

My friend Michel Kelly-Gagnon of the Montreal Economic Institute echoes the horrid news about Cuba's economy.

> As anyone who has spent any amount of time in Cuba outside the tourist compounds can tell you, socialism, particularly the unsubsidized version that we have seen since the fall of the Soviet empire, has been a disaster. …The hospitals which supposedly offer free care only do so quickly and effectively to the politically connected, friends and family of staff members, and to those who pay the largest bribes… That "free" university education that many Cubans get in technical fields is rarely worth much more than what students pay for it. There are few books in the country's schools, and those that can be found are years, if not decades old. The country's libraries are empty… The guaranteed jobs that all Cubans have are fine, until you realize that the average salary is in the range of $20 a month. Worse, the food and other staple allotments that Cubans have long felt entitled to, have shrunk over the years. Tourists often marvel at how thin and healthy Cubans look. Sadly many of them are outright hungry.

Though Michel includes a bit of optimism in his column, pointing out that there's been a modest bit of economic liberalization (a point that I've also made, even to the point of joking about whether we should trade Obama for Castro).

> Communist Cuba, beset with an oppressive bureaucracy, an anachronistic cradle-to-grave welfare state, a hopelessly subpar economy, and widespread poverty, is gradually shifting to private sector solutions. Starting when Raul Castro "temporarily" took

over power from his brother Fidel six years ago and culminating with the Communist party's approval of a major package of reforms…, Cuba has taken a series of increasingly bold steps to implement free market reforms. These range from providing entrepreneurs with increased flexibility to run small businesses, and use of state agricultural lands by individual farmers, to the elimination of a variety of burdensome rules and regulations. Ironically, there is a lot that Canadians…can learn from that shift.

And there's a lot the United States can learn, particularly our President, who is so deluded that he said there are (presumably positive) things America can learn from Cuba.

One common talking point from Cuban sympathizers is that the country has done a good job of reducing infant mortality. But, as Johan Norberg explains, that claim largely evaporates upon closer examination.

The bottom line is that communism is a system that is grossly inconsistent with both human freedom and economic liberty.

And because it squashes economic liberty (thanks to central planning, price controls, and the various other features of total statism), that ensures mass poverty.

Amazingly, there are still some leftists who want us to believe that communism would work if "good people" were in charge. I guess they don't understand that good people, by definition, don't want to control the lives of others.

P.S. No analysis of Cuba would be complete without noting the bizarre fetish of some leftists to wear t-shirts celebrating the homicidal racist Che Guevara. What's next, baseball caps featuring Kim Jong-un. Computer screen savers featuring Hermann Göring?

Pol Pot bobble head dolls?

There are some sick weirdos in this world to defend any form of coercive statism.

P.S. Here's my only communist-themed joke(other than the video of Reagan's jokes about communism).

P.P.S. At the advice of a reader, let me add one more point. Probably the most amazing indictment of communism is that living standards in Cuba when Castro took power were about even with living standards in Hong Kong. Today, the gap between the two is enormous.

ENVY, FAIRNESS, REDISTRIBUTION, COMPASSION, AND MORALITY

AUGUST 2, 2017

I confess that I'm never sure how best to persuade and educate people about the value of limited government.

Is it best to make a moral and philosophical case against state coercion?

Or is it best to make a practical case that a free society produces greater prosperity?

Regular readers presumably will put me in the second camp since most of my columns involve data and evidence on the superior outcomes associated with markets compared to statism.

That being said, I actually don't think we will prevail until and unless we can convince people that it is ethically wrong to use government power to dictate and control the lives of other people.

So I'm always trying to figure out what motivates people and how they decide what policies to support.

With this in mind, I was very interested to see that nine scholars from five continents (North America, South America, Europe, Asia, and Australia), representing six countries (Canada, United States, Argentina, Netherlands, Israel, and Australia) and four disciplines (psychology, criminology, economics, and anthropology), produced a major study on what motivates support for redistribution.

> Why do people support economic redistribution? …By economic redistribution, we mean the modification of a distribution of

resources across a population as the result of a political process. ...it is worthwhile to understand how distributive policies are mapped into and refracted through our evolved psychological mechanisms.

The study explain how human evolution may impact our attitudes, a topic that I addressed back in 2010.

The human mind has been organized by natural selection to respond to evolutionarily recurrent challenges and opportunities pertaining to the social distribution of resources, as well as other social interactions. ...For example, it was hypothesized that modern welfare activates the evolved forager risk-pooling psychology — a psychology that causes humans to be more motivated to share when individual productivity is subject to chance-driven interruptions, and less motivated to share when they think they are being exploited by low-effort free riders. Ancestrally, sharing resources that came in unsynchronized, high-variance, large packages (e.g., large game) allowed individuals to buffer each other's shortfalls at low additional cost.

Here's how the authors structured their research.

...we propose that the mind perceives modern redistribution as an ancestral game or scene featuring three notional players: the needy other, the better-off other, and the actor herself. ...we use the existence of individual differences in compassion, self-interest, and envy as a research tool for investigating the joint contribution of these motivational systems to forming attitudes about redistribution.

And here's how they conducted their research.

We conducted 13 studies with 6,024 participants in four countries to test the hypothesis that compassion, envy, and self-interest jointly predict support for redistribution.

Participants completed instruments measuring their (i) support for redistribution; (ii) dispositional compassion; (iii) dispositional envy; (iv) expected personal gain or loss from redistribution (our measure of self-interest); (v) political party identification; (vi) aid given personally to the poor; (vii) wealthy-harming preferences; (viii) endorsement of pro-cedural fairness; (ix) endorsement of distributional fairness; (x) age; (xi) gender; and (xii) socioeconomic status (SES).

Now let's look at some of the findings, starting with the fact that personal compassion is not associated with support for coerced redistribution. Indeed, advocates of government redistribution tend to be less generous (a point that I've previously noted).

> Consider personally aiding the poor—as distinct from supporting state-enacted redistribution. Participants in the United States, India, and the United Kingdom (studies 1a–c) were asked whether they had given money, food, or other material resources of their own to the poor during the last 12 mo; 74–90% of the participants had. …dispositional compassion was the only reliable predictor of giving aid to the poor. A unit increase in dispositional compassion is associated with 161%, 361%, and 96% increased odds of having given aid to the poor in the United States, India, and the United Kingdom. …Interestingly, support for government redistribution was not a unique predictor of personally aiding the poor in the regressions… Support for government redistribution is not aiding the needy writ large—in the United States, data from the General Social Survey indicate that support for redistribution is associated with lower charitable contributions to religious and nonreligious causes (61). Unlike supporting redistribution, aiding the needy is predicted by compassion alone.

But here's the most shocking part of the results.

The people motivated by envy are often interested in hurting those above them than they are in helping those below them.

> ...consider envy. Participants in the United States, India, and the United Kingdom (studies 1a–c) were given two hypothetical scenarios and asked to indicate their preferred one. In one scenario, the wealthy pay an additional 10% in taxes, and the poor receive an additional sum of money. In the other scenario, the wealthy pay an additional 50% in taxes (i.e., a tax increment five times greater than in the first scenario), and the poor receive (only) one-half the additional amount that they receive in the first scenario. That is, higher taxes paid by the wealthy yielded relatively less money for the poor, and vice versa... Fourteen percent to 18% of the American, Indian, and British participants indicated a preference for the scenario featuring a higher tax rate for the wealthy even though it produced less money to help the poor (SI Appendix, Table S3). We regressed this wealthy-harming preference simultaneously on support for redistribution... Dispositional envy was the only reliable predictor. A unit increase in envy is associated with 23%, 47%, and 43% greater odds of preferring the wealthy-harming scenario in the United States, India, and the United Kingdom.

This is astounding, in a very bad way.

It means that there really are people who are willing to deprive poor people so long as they can hurt rich people.

Even though I have shared polling data echoing these findings, I still have a hard time accepting that some people think like that.

But the data in this study seem to confirm Margaret Thatcher's observation about what really motivates the left.

The authors have a more neutral way of saying this. They simply point out that compassion and envy can lead to very different results.

Compassion and envy motivate the attainment of different ends. Compassion, but not envy, predicts personally helping the poor. Envy, but not compassion, predicts a desire to tax the wealthy even when that costs the poor.

Since we're on the topic or morality, markets, and statism, my colleague Ryan Bourne wrote an interesting column for *CapX* looking at research on what type of system brings out the best in people.

It turns out that markets promote cooperation and trust.

> …experimental work of Herbert Gintis, who has analysed the behaviours of 15 tribal societies from around the world, including "hunter-gatherers, horticulturalists, nomadic herders, and small-scale sedentary farmers — in Africa, Latin America, and Asia." Playing a host of economic games, Gintis found that societies exposed to voluntary exchange through markets were more highly motivated by non-financial fairness considerations than those which were not. "The notion that the market economy makes people greedy, selfish, and amoral is simply fallacious," Gintis concluded. …Gintis again summarises, "movements for religious and lifestyle tolerance, gender equality, and democracy have flourished and triumphed in societies governed by market exchange, and nowhere else."

Whereas greater government control and intervention produce a zero-sum mentality and cheating.

> …we might expect greed, cheating and intolerance to be more prevalent in societies where individuals can only fulfil selfish desires by taking from, overpowering or using dominant political or hierarchical positions to rule over and extort from others. Markets actually encourage collaboration and exchange between parties that might otherwise not interact. This interdependency discourages violence and builds trust and tolerance. …In a 2014

paper, economists tested Berlin residents' willingness to cheat in a simple game involving rolling die, whereby self-reported scores could lead to small monetary pay-offs. Participants presented passports and ID cards to the researchers, which allowed them to assess their backgrounds. The results were clear: participants from an East German family background were far more likely to cheat than those from the West. What is more, the "longer individuals were exposed to socialism, the more likely they were to cheat."

All of which brings me back to where I started.

How do you persuade people to favor liberty if they are somehow wired to have a zero-sum view of the world and they think that goal of public policy is to tear down the rich, even if that hurts the poor?

Though the internal inconsistency of the previous sentence maybe points to the problem. If the poor and the rich are both hurt by a policy (or if both benefit from a policy), then the world clearly isn't zero-sum. And we now from voluminous evidence, of course, that the world isn't that way.

But how to convince people, other than making the same arguments over and over again?

ABOUT THE AUTHOR

A public policy economist in Washington Dan Mitchell was a Senior Fellow at the Cato Institute, a Senior Fellow at the Heritage Foundation, an economist for Senator Bob Packwood and the Senate Finance Committee, and a Director of Tax and Budget Policy at Citizens for a Sound Economy. He is currently the Chairman for the Center for Freedom and Prosperity.

He Blogs @ https://danieljmitchell.wordpress.com